Let's Wonder About Science

SOLIDS, LIQUIDS AND GASES

J.M. Patten, Ed.D.

The Rourke Book Co., Inc.
Vero Beach, Florida 32964

PHOTO CREDITS
All photos © J.M. Patten

Library of Congress Cataloging-in-Publication Data

Patten, J.M., 1944-
    Solids, liquids and gases / J.M. Patten.
    p. cm. — (Let's wonder about science)
    Includes index.
    ISBN 1-55916-126-4
    1. Matter—Composition—Juvenile literature. 2. Matter—Properties—
Juvenile literature. [1. Matter.] I. Title. II. Series: Patten, J.M., 1994-
Let's wonder about science.
QC173.16.P37 1995
530.4—dc20   94-47599
                                            CIP
                                            AC

Printed in the USA

TABLE OF CONTENTS

WHAT IS SCIENCE?

Young scientists like you have always enjoyed finding out about **solids, liquids** and **gases.** They can do all kinds of fun tricks.

Solids, liquids and gases are colorful names of some everyday things. You already know a lot about ice, water and steam, and they're a big part of this science story.

Let's read all about solids, liquids and gases, and find out much more.

This cat is wondering about glass. Glass is a solid form of matter you can see through.

KINDS OF MATTER

Here's a tricky question. How are a candy bar, a puddle and a gust of wind alike?

Of course—they are all forms of **matter.** Matter is anything that takes up space—like candy bars, puddles and the wind.

The spilled soda is out of the glass. It spreads every which way and into puddle shapes.

Water is flowing from these three pipes with great force and speed.

Here's an easier question. How are they different? Candy bars are good for eating, puddles are good for splashing, and wind is always good for flying a kite.

They're also different because a candy bar is a solid, a puddle is a liquid and wind is a gas. Now this is interesting.

THE BIG THREE

All matter fits into one of three groups. Let's think of these as "the big three" so they will be easy to remember.

The big three are solids, liquids and gases. Scientists call these groups the **three states of matter.**

Sometimes these terms are confusing. The "gas" that runs your car or boat is a nickname for gasoline, and is really a liquid. When scientists talk about a gas, they never mean gasoline.

Gas that goes in your car is not really a gas. Gasoline is a liquid.

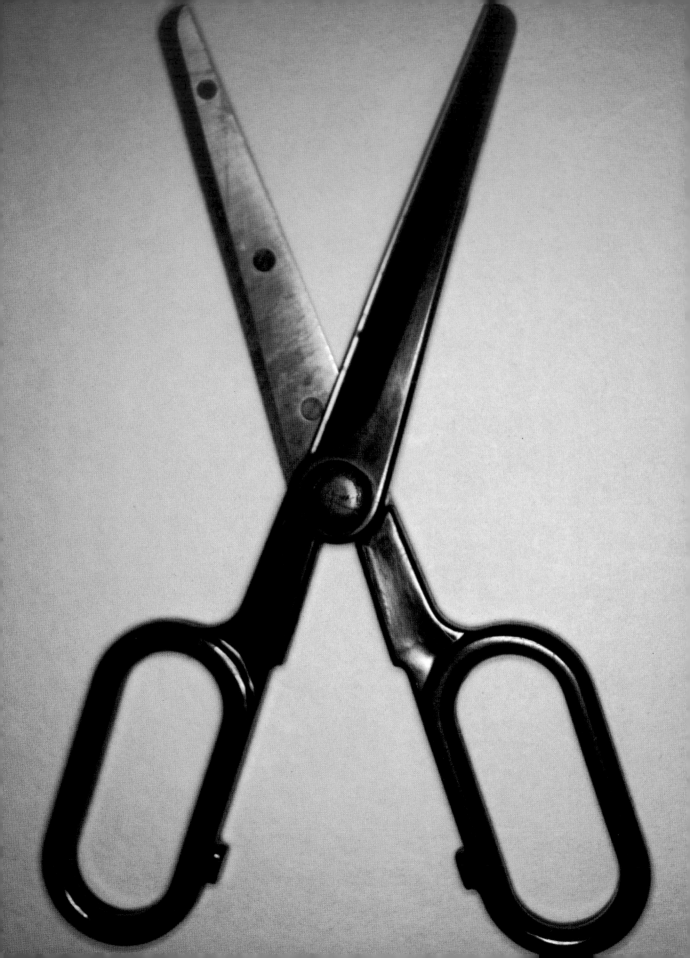

TINY THINGS CALLED MOLECULES

All matter is made from tiny particles, or bits, called **molecules.** Molecules bond, or join together, in special ways to make all kinds of different things.

People can say that candy bars are made from candy molecules. Puddles are made from water molecules, and the wind is made up of air molecules.

Don't worry—molecules cannot bond in weird ways to make strange new things. All molecules must follow nature's rules. They can only join together to make the solids, liquids and gases they have always made.

Scissors are used to cut solids. You don't need tools to cut liquids or gases.

SOLIDS—HARD AS A ROCK

Molecules in solid matter like paper clips, dishes, baseball bats, mountains and books are packed very, very close together.

Solids feel hard because the molecules inside are right next to each other. They don't have space to move around.

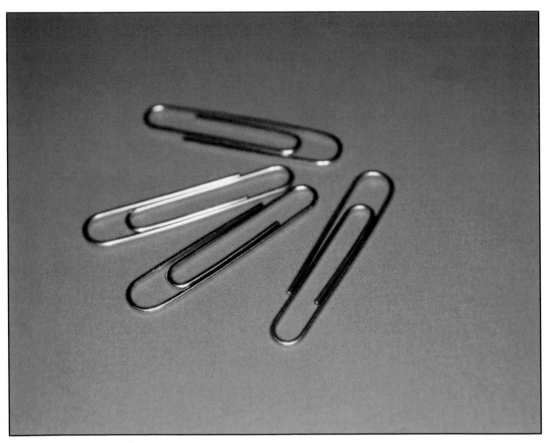

Paper clips cannot move or bend by themselves. They are a solid state, or form, of matter.

Stamps aren't very thick or heavy, but they are a solid state of matter.

Solids all have a shape of their own. Your pencil will look the same tomorrow as it does today. *You* can break it in half and change its shape, but the *pencil* cannot change shape by itself.

Also, solid matter stays put until someone or something moves it. For example, sand is solid matter. Waves can move the sand on the beach, but the sand cannot move itself.

LIQUIDS—MATTER ON THE MOVE

Liquids like chocolate syrup, molasses, apple juice and water are another form of matter. Molecules in liquids are not packed together as tightly as in solids. Liquid matter can flow, or move, because liquid molecules have room to move around.

Rain splashes down, and waves roll up and down. You can walk through water because your feet can push liquid water molecules out of the way. You can't walk through a tree. Solid tree molecules cannot be pushed around.

Liquids have no shape of their own. They are shaped by the lake bed, river banks, bottles or cups they are in. Milk has the shape of its carton. If you pour it into a glass, the shape changes. If you spill it, it spreads out every which way.

Sand is a solid state of matter and cannot move by itself. The waves are moving the sand around the feet.

GASES—CATCH ME IF YOU CAN

Gas is the third form of matter. Gas molecules are even farther apart than liquid molecules. You can pour liquids, but gases float around and spread out in all directions.

If you take a deep breath and blow up a balloon, you fill it with a gas called air. Air fills all the empty space in the world.

When you move, you push air, gaseous matter, all around. Air is the gas you feel when you fan your face or go fast on your bike.

Oxygen and nitrogen are gases you can't see or smell. Chlorine, a gas used to kill germs in water, is green and harmful to breathe. Helium is a gas that rises and makes balloons float. There is even a gas that stinks like rotten eggs, called sulphur.

These balloons are filled with a gaseous matter called helium—a gas that rises.

CHANGING FORMS OF MATTER

Let's wonder—can a solid become a liquid? Can a liquid become a solid? Can a liquid become a gas? This could be lots of fun!

The answer, of course, is yes.

Ice forms when water freezes. Ice is the solid state, or form, of water.

Steam forms when water boils. Steam is the gaseous state of water.

Matter can change from solid to liquid to gas. It can even do it backwards. The reasons are easy to understand, and you see it happen every day.

All that is needed to change the form of matter is a change in temperature. Making matter hotter or colder will change the form it is in. Scientists call these *changes of state*. We also call them **freezing, melting** and **boiling.**

ICE, WATER AND STEAM

Ice is a solid. Water is a liquid. Steam is a gas. They are three different forms of the same kind of matter. How can this be?

The science magic that changes matter into its different forms is heat. Let's find out how this works.

When water is put in a very cold place—like the north pole—heat is taken away. The liquid water turns into a solid—ice. Scientists call this freezing.

Ice put in the warm sun gets heat back. It becomes liquid. Solid matter becomes liquid matter when it is heated. This is called melting.

Now let's really heat the water up. As the liquid gets hotter and hotter, it turns into a gas named steam. This is called boiling.

Thermometers tell temperature. All you need to change the form of matter is a change in temperature.

GLOSSARY

boiling (BOYL ing) — the point at which heat makes liquid bubble and turn into a gas

freezing (FREEZ ing) — the point at which cold turns liquid into a solid

gas (GASS) — the form of matter without shape or volume

liquid (LI kwid) — the form of matter in which the molecules flow

matter (MAT er) — every living and nonliving thing that takes up space

melting (MELT ing) — the point at which heat changes a solid to a liquid

molecule (MAHL eh kyool) — tiny particles formed by two or more different kinds of atoms joined together

solid (SAH lid) — the form of matter that has its own shape

three states of matter (THREE STAYTS uhv MAT er) — solid, liquid or gas

Liquids have no shape of their own. They become the shape of whatever they are in.

23

INDEX